Feast and Gratitude

Grace T. Hollis

Copyright Notice

© 2025 Grace T. Hollis

All rights reserved. No part of this publication may be reproduced, stored in a retrieval system, or transmitted in any form or by any means—electronic, mechanical, photocopying, recording, or otherwise—without the prior written permission of the author, except for brief quotations in reviews or articles.

Publisher Information

Grace T. Hollis Catering & Publishing

Disclaimer

The recipes and techniques in this book are provided for informational and educational purposes only. While every effort has been made to ensure accuracy, the author and publisher assume no responsibility for adverse reactions to foods or beverages prepared using these recipes. Nutritional information, cooking times, and ingredient measurements are approximate and can vary based on equipment, ingredient brands, and environmental factors. Readers are advised to exercise proper food safety practices, including cooking foods to safe internal temperatures and handling ingredients in a sanitary manner.

TABLE OF CONTENTS

- **5**   INTRODUCTION
- **12.**   THE CLASSICS REVISITED
- **32.**   MODERN TWIST ON TRADITION
- **48**   FRIENDLY DIETARY TABLE
- **56.**   LEFTOVERS REIMAGINED
- **62.**   BEVERAGE PAIRING AND TOASTS
- **72.**   THE ART OF HOSTING
- **86.**   HAPPY THANKSGIVING NOTES

IFEAST & GRATITUDE IS THE ULTIMATE THANKSGIVING RECIPE BOOK WITH EASY RECIPES, HOSTING MUST-HAVES, DINNER PARTY TIPS, AND CREATIVE IDEAS FOR HOME ENTERTAINING

Trademarks & Acknowledgments

All brand names and product names used in this book are trademarks, registered trademarks, or trade names of their respective holders. Use of them does not imply any affiliation with or endorsement by them.

Special thanks to the recipe testers, photographers, and designers whose contributions made this book possible:

Photography: Aisling Byrne

Food Styling: Martin O'Leary

Cover & Interior Design: Fiona McCarthy

First Edition: May 2025

A Feast of Gratitude

The table is where memory and meaning meet.

Author's Note
The Story Behind the Table

The first smell that hits me every year isn't the turkey—it's the sage. That earthy, unmistakable aroma that instantly transports me back to my grandmother's kitchen, where she stirred stuffing by hand in a bowl the size of a washtub. No recipe, no measurements—just muscle memory and love.

I remember the year I hosted my first Thanksgiving. I burned the pie, undercooked the turkey, and forgot to set the table until ten minutes before guests arrived. But we laughed, we ate (eventually), and we made memories that still surface at every holiday since. What I've learned is that Thanksgiving isn't about pulling off a flawless meal—it's about showing up, setting the table, and welcoming people in.

Over the years, my Thanksgiving table has grown and shifted. It's held Southern casseroles, Middle Eastern salads, gluten-free rolls, vegan roasts, and at least one tofu turkey that still sparks heated debate in our family group chat. What stays the same is the heart of it: gathering with intention, cooking with care, and honoring both the old and the new.

> ## My First Thanksgiving Disaster
>
> "I burned the pie, undercooked the turkey, and dropped the gravy—but somehow, it was still the most perfect Thanksgiving I've ever had."

This book is a love letter to that spirit. To the dishes we make every year because someone's eyes light up when they see them. To the new recipes that surprise and delight. To the tables where stories are shared, glasses are raised, and gratitude isn't just spoken—it's tasted. Whether you're a first-time host, a seasoned pro, or just showing up with a store-bought pie and a bottle of wine (bless you), this book is your companion. Together, we'll craft a Thanksgiving feast that feels like home—whatever that looks like to you.

Thanksgiving THEN & NOW
A Brief History

THEN	NOW
Rooted In Indigenous harvest traditions	Celebrated by a diverse, multicultural America
1621 Wampanoag and Pilgrim gathering often cited as "the "first"	Recognized as more complex than textbook myths
Thanksgiving formalized by Lincoln in 1863 during the Civil War	A national holiday that reflects evolving values and voices
Regional staples emerged over time: cornbread, oysters, wild rice	Global flavors now grace the table: jollof rice, tamales, halal roasts
Centered on a singular, traditional narrative	Embraces many stories, cultures, and customs
A meal of shared harvest and historical reflection	A moment for gratitude, chosen family, inclusivity, and renewal
Often framed as a solemn tradition	Celebrated with creativity, personalization, and cultural pride

Thanksgiving didn't begin with stuffing and cranberry sauce. Its roots lie in the harvest festivals of Indigenous peoples, long before the Plymouth settlers ever set foot in America.

While the 1621 gathering between the Wampanoag and Pilgrims is often cited as the "first Thanksgiving," the truth —complex, painful, and powerful—is far more nuanced than the myths we learned in school. It wasn't until 1863, in the midst of the Civil War, that President Abraham Lincoln proclaimed Thanksgiving a national holiday.

Over time, regional flavors crept into the table: cornbread in the South, oysters in the Northeast, wild rice in the Midwest. And today? Thanksgiving reflects the rich mosaic of America itself. You'll find jollof rice next to the turkey, tamales tucked between stuffing and greens, and tables that are entirely plant-based or entirely halal. What hasn't changed is the heart of the day: gratitude.

However you celebrate, and whatever your table looks like, Thanksgiving remains a moment to pause, gather, reflect, and feast.

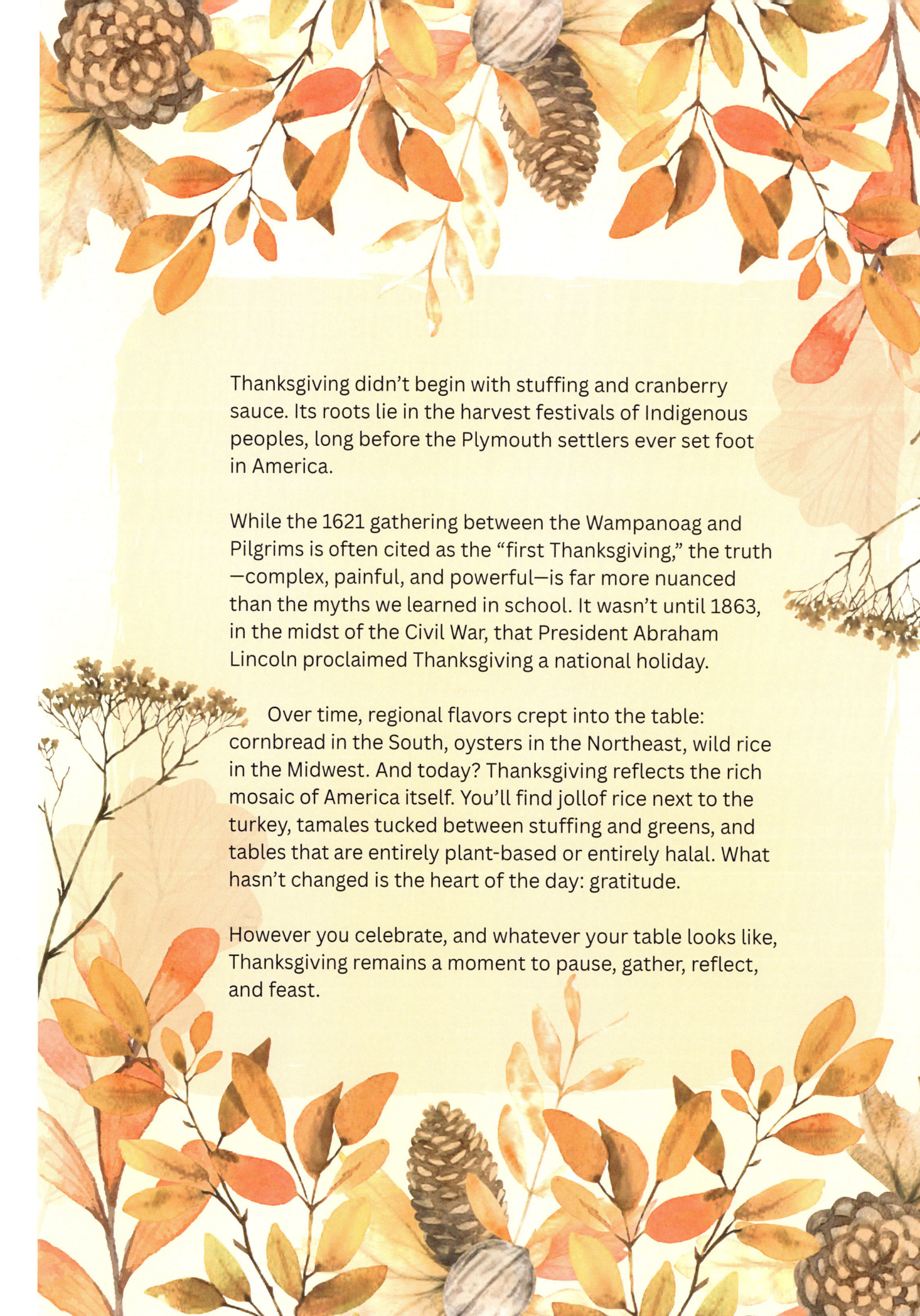

The best Thanksgiving meals aren't flawless. They're full-hearted

Warmth

Not just from the oven, but from the way people lean in, share stories, pass plates, and say things like "remember when..."

The most unforgettable Thanksgiving meals aren't the ones where the turkey is perfectly golden or the rolls rise just right. They're the ones where someone brought their whole heart to the table.

Sometimes it's chaos. There's the dog eating half the pie. The kids spilling cranberry sauce. The moment when someone quietly sets a plate for the person who isn't with us this year. That, to me, is Thanksgiving.

This year, I want my Thanksgiving table to feel.....

_____

How to Use This Book

A joyful guide to navigating your Thanksgiving feast

This book is organized to help you plan, cook, and celebrate with joy and confidence. Inside, you'll find delicious recipes, spanning timeless classics and bold new favourites

Make-Ahead
Recipes you can prep ahead for stress-free hosting

Vegan/Vegeterian
Plant-based or adaptable dishes

Kid-Friendly
Recipes little hands can help with

Wine Pairing Included
Perfect drinks for each dish

One-Pot/Sheet Pan
Minimal mess, maximum flavor

Choose Your Own Feast Adventure

- Build a full menu from one chapter (like Dietary-Friendly Table or Regional Celebrations)
- Mix and match to create a celebration that's truly yours

Use the Chapter 5 planner to prep ahead and stay cairn in the chaos

Thanksgiving isn't about perfection-it's about presence.

So don't worry if the turkey's dry or the pie cracks in the oven. Light a candle. Laugh it off. Fill your plate, raise your glass, and savor the moment- because this is what makes a feast.

The Classics Revisited

Foundational recipes every Thanksgiving table needs—with flavor-forward updates, time-saving tips, and just the right touch of modern magic.

Herb-Roasted Turkey with Pan Drippings
Your centerpiece bird, elevated. Crisp skin, juicy meat, and foolproof flavor from an herby compound butter.

Cornbread & Sage Stuffing
A soul-warming Southern classic with buttery onions and fresh sage, baked golden and fluffy.

Mashed Potatoes with Brown Butter
The comfort you expect, deepened with nutty brown butter and roasted garlic.

Classic Green Bean Casserole from Scratch
Fresh green beans, real mushrooms, and a silky béchamel topped with crisp shallots.

Perfect Apple Pie with Cheddar Crust
Sweet, tart, buttery, and bold. The cheddar crust nods to Northeast tradition.

Homemade Cranberry-Orange Relish
Tangy and bright with citrus, ready in ten minutes—perfect for turkey or sandwiches.

Grandma's Pumpkin Pie
Updated with maple warmth and a flaky crust. Cozy meets timeless.

> Every family has their "no-matter-what" dishes. What are yours? Jot them down—and maybe add a new one!
> _____
> _____
> _____

Foundational recipes every Thanksgiving table needs

If Thanksgiving had a core memory, this would be it. Golden roast turkey, silky mashed potatoes, tart cranberry sauce, and pies that perfume the whole house—these are the sacred hallmarks of the holiday. But that doesn't mean they can't evolve. Think of this chapter as a greatest hits album... remastered.

Whether you're hosting your first feast or perfecting your twentieth, these dishes are your foundation—now smarter, simpler, and more sensational than ever.

Think of this chapter as a greatest hits album... remastered.

The heart of each dish is still there, but we've dialed up the flavor, streamlined the technique, and added a few brilliant flourishes that make hosting easier and eating even more joyful.

Whether this is your first Thanksgiving in charge or your twentieth turkey triumph, these are the recipes that anchor the holiday. Timeless, dependable, and just a little bit magical.

Sidebars & Pro Tips

- **Turkey Carving** 101
  Step-by-step visuals and knife know-how.
- **Gravy Troubleshooting**
  Lumpy? Too thin? No drippings? Solved.
- **Pie Crust Guide**
  Rolling, crimping, blind baking—plus gluten-free options.

What You'll Learn in This Chapter

- How to balance salt, acid, and richness for crowd-pleasing flavor
- Simple upgrades that make nostalgic dishes shine
- Timing tips so every dish hits the table warm and ready
- Confidence in the "big stuff"—yes, you can master the turkey and pies

Herb-Roasted TURKEY WITH PAN DRIPPINGS

This is the bird that built Thanksgiving — only better. Crispy skin, juicy meat, and herby butter tucked beneath the skin make it unforgettable. No stress. No dryness. Just glory.

This is the turkey that convinced my family to stop begging for ham

NOTES:

Turkey Carving

- **Let It Rest** 20–30 minutes
- **Sharp Tools Only** Chef's knife > serrated.
- **No Slip Zone** - Damp towel under carving board.
- **Legs First.** Cut at the joint, not the bone.
- **Then the Breasts.** Slice along the breastbone, then across the grain.
- **Wishbone Trick.** Remove it early. Carving's smoother.

INGREDIENTS

- 1 whole turkey (12–14 lbs), thawed
- ½ cup unsalted butter, softened
- 2 tbsp chopped fresh rosemary
- 2 tbsp chopped thyme
- 2 tbsp chopped sage
- 1 tbsp kosher salt
- 1 tsp black pepper
- 1 onion, quartered
- 1 lemon, halved
- 4 cups chicken or turkey stock (for pan drippings)

Let the turkey rest for at least 30 minutes before carving. It keeps every bite juicy.

🍖 Servings: 10–12

⏱ Prep Time: 30 minutes

🔥 Cook Time: 3.5–4 hours
   (for 12–14 lb turkey at 15 min/lb)

🌿 Rest Time: 30 minutes

DIRECTIONS

- Preheat oven to 325°F.
- Mix butter with herbs, salt, and pepper.
- Loosen turkey skin and spread butter underneath.
- Stuff cavity with onion and lemon. Tie legs.
- Roast turkey on a rack, basting occasionally, until internal temp reaches 165°F (approx. 15 min/lb).
- Let rest 30 minutes. Save drippings for gravy.

CORNBREAD STUFFING & Sage

Southern comfort at its finest — sweet, savory, buttery, and deeply satisfying. A classic reborn in golden, crispy-edged form.

Bake your cornbread a day ahead. It crumbles better and absorbs more flavor

NOTES:

Stuffing Secrets

- **Dry cornbread** = better texture. Day-old is golden.
- **Sauté low and slow.** Onions + celery should melt, not brown.
- **Herbs make the dish.** Fresh sage is non-negotiable.
- **Eggs bind it.** Skip them, and you'll have a crumble, not a stuffing.
- **Don't pack it down.** Looser stuffing = fluffier results.
- **Let it rest.** Just 10 minutes makes slicing easier and keeps it steamy.

INGREDIENTS

- 6 cups cubed cornbread (preferably day-old)
- 1 cup diced onion
- 1 cup diced celery
- ½ cup butter
- 2 tbsp fresh sage, minced
- 1 tsp dried thyme
- 2½ cups chicken broth
- 2 eggs, beaten
- Salt and pepper to taste

Don't overmix.
A loose toss keeps the stuffing fluffy.

- Servings: 10–12
- Prep Time: 30 minutes
- Cook Time: 30–35 minutes
- Rest Time: 5–10 minutes before serving

DIRECTIONS

- Preheat oven to 350°F. Grease a 9x13" dish.
- Sauté onion and celery in butter until soft. Stir in sage and thyme.
- In a large bowl, combine cornbread, sautéed veg, broth, eggs, and seasoning.
- Gently mix and pour into the dish.
- Bake uncovered for 30–35 minutes or until golden brown.

FLAVOR
BALANCING SALT, ACID & RICHNESS

How to layer flavor like a pro — without overwhelming the classics.

Salt
- Enhances, rounds, and unlocks flavor.
- Try: kosher salt, cheese, broth, soy sauce, miso
- Cornbread Stuffing, Mashed Potatoes, Apple Pie Crust

Acid
- Cuts through richness and wakes up the palate.
- Try: citrus juice/zest, vinegar, cranberry, fermented foods
- Cranberry-Orange Relish, Apple Pie (lemon), Balsamic Roasted Veg

Richness
- Adds comfort and depth — just don't let it dominate.
- Try: butter, cream, egg yolk, nuts, browned sauces
- Pumpkin Pie, Brown Butter Potatoes, Pan Gravy

Pro Tip
- Aim for balance on the whole plate, not just each dish. If your mains are rich, let sides bring brightness

THANKSGIVNG TIMING CHEAT SHEET

A CALM KITCHEN IS A HAPPY KITCHEN.

Up to 3 Days Ahead

- Make cranberry relish
- Bake cornbread for stuffing
- Prep pie dough + refrigerate
- Chop veggies for mirepoix/base

1–2 Days Ahead

- Assemble stuffing (bake day of)
- Bake pies (Pumpkin holds beautifully)
- Make compound butter for turkey
- Pre-make gravy base or stock

Thanksgiving Morning

- Roast turkey (start early!)
- Brown butter + roast garlic for mash
- Assemble green bean casserole
- Roll pie crust + bake apple pie (optional)

1 Hour Before Dinner

- Reheat sides (375°F is your magic number)
- Mash potatoes first — they hold heat well
- Carve turkey, tent with foil
- Light candles, cue music, pour drinks

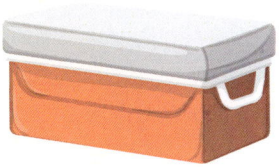

Pro Tip

Want everything warm? Use a cooler as a warming box. Just line it with foil and fill with hot dishes.

Mashed POTATOES WITH BROWN BUTTER

These aren't your everyday mashed potatoes. They're luxurious, nutty, rich — and made for the holiday table. The browned butter adds depth, the roasted garlic whispers comfort, and every bite is a reminder that simplicity can still be show-stopping.

Roast the garlic while the potatoes boil. It makes your kitchen smell divine — and your guests might start hovering

NOTES:

Potato Perfection

- Use Yukon Golds for a naturally creamy texture — no need for heavy cream.
- Roast the garlic while the potatoes boil. It adds depth and saves time.
- Warm the milk before mashing — it blends better and keeps potatoes hot.
- Don't overmix or they'll get gluey. Mash just until smooth.
- Brown butter = game changer. Nutty, rich, unforgettable.

INGREDIENTS

- 3 lbs potatoes, peeled and cubed
- ¾ cup whole milk (warm)
- ½ cup unsalted butter
- 4 cloves garlic, roasted and mashed
- Salt and pepper, to taste

Servings: 6 - 8

Prep Time: 10 minutes

Cook Time: 20 minutes

Rest Time: 5 minutes (just to let the flavors settle before serving)

Brown butter can go from golden to burnt in seconds. Swirl the pan and trust your nose — when it smells toasty and nutty, it's ready.

DIRECTIONS

- Boil potatoes until fork-tender, 15–20 minutes. Drain well.
- Brown the butter in a saucepan over medium heat until golden and nutty. Remove from heat.
- Mash potatoes with warm milk, roasted garlic, and brown butter (reserve a little for drizzling).
- Season with salt and pepper. Taste and adjust.
- Serve warm, drizzled with extra brown butter and optional herbs.

Classic GREENBEAN CASSEROLE *from Scratch*

Forget the cans. Forget the gloopy stuff. This version brings in crisp-tender green beans, real mushrooms, a dreamy homemade béchamel, and a golden blanket of crispy shallots. All the comfort, none of the compromise.

Real mushrooms and béchamel make all the difference. Once you go from-scratch, you won't go back.

Quick Tips

- Blanch first for vibrant color and perfect texture.
- Skip the cans — fresh mushrooms + béchamel = magic.
- Add soy sauce for deep, savory umami.
- Make ahead and reheat — it holds up beautifully.
- Crispy shallots on top? Non-negotiable.

This dish holds well — perfect to make ahead and reheat. Serve alongside turkey and stuffing, or pair with a fresh salad for balance

NOTES:

INGREDIENTS

- 1 lb green beans, trimmed
- 8 oz mushrooms, sliced (cremini or button)
- 2 tbsp unsalted butter
- 2 tbsp all-purpose flour
- 1½ cups whole milk, warmed
- 1 tsp soy sauce (adds umami depth)
- Salt and pepper, to taste
- 1 cup crispy shallots (store-bought or homemade)

Servings: 6-8

Prep Time: 20 minutes

Cook Time: 25 minutes

Rest Time: 5 minutes

**Blanch first!
It locks in color, texture,
and that perfect snap.**

DIRECTIONS

- Boil green beans in salted water for 3 minutes until bright green.
- Put beans in ice water, drain, and pat dry.
- Make the sauce: Sauté mushrooms in butter until golden (6-8 mins).
- Stir in flour and cook 1 min. Whisk in warm milk, soy sauce, salt, and pepper.
- Simmer until thick.
- Assemble: Toss green beans with sauce in a greased 9x9-inch baking dish.
- Cover with crispy shallots. Bake at 375°F for 20-25 minutes, until bubbling and golden.

Homemade CRANBERRY ORANGE RELISH

A Ruby-red relish with just the right balance of bright citrus and tangy berries, to cut through the richness like a charm — It takes about 10 minutes from start to finish. Even better? It's the hero of the day-after turkey sandwich.

This is the only "sauce" I'd eat with a spoon straight from the fridge.

NOTES:

Quick Tips

- Zest first, then juice. It's way easier that way.
- Don't walk away. Cranberries pop fast—stay nearby.
- Cool it down. Sauce thickens as it cools—don't overcook.
- Make ahead. Flavors deepen overnight in the fridge.
- Leftover magic. Add to sandwiches, oatmeal, even cocktails.

INGREDIENTS

- 12 oz fresh cranberries (about 3 cups)
- ½ cup orange juice (freshly squeezed is best)
- Zest of 1 orange
- ⅔ cup granulated sugar
- Pinch of salt

Servings: 2 cups (Serves 6–8 as a side)

Prep Time: 5 minutes

Cook Time: 8–10 minutes

Rest Time: 15–20 minutes to cool

Don't overcook!
Cranberries pop fast — stop when they're just-softened for the best texture.

DIRECTIONS

- Combine all ingredients in a medium saucepan on medium heat.
- Cook, stirring occasionally, for 8–10 minutes — just until the cranberries pop and the mixture begins to thicken.
- Remove from heat and let cool to room temperature. The sauce will continue to thicken as it cools.
- Transfer to a bowl or jar, cover, and refrigerate. It keeps beautifully for up to 1 week — and it's even better the next day.

GRAVY
Fixes & Flavor Boosters

- **Lumpy?**

Whisk hard, strain, or use an immersion blender.

- **Too Thin?**

Simmer to reduce or add a cornstarch slurry.

- **Too Thick?**

Stir in warm stock or water gradually.

- **Too Salty?**

Add cream, broth, or a pinch of sugar.

- **No Drippings?**

Use stock + sautéed aromatics for flavor.

- **Looks Dull?**

A splash of soy or vinegar brightens it up.

- **Flat or Bland?**

Add a splash of Worcestershire sauce or a dab of Dijon mustard for umami depth.

- **Too Pale?**

Whisk in a spoonful of dark soy or roast a tablespoon of flour for color and richness.

- **Gravy Split?**

Broken or greasy? Emulsify it back together with a quick whisk and a splash of cream or butter.

- **Want a deeper flavor?**

Sauté shallots, garlic, or a spoon of tomato paste in your fat before adding flour.

PIE CRUST GUIDE

- EDGE CRIMPING
- TOP CRUST
- VENTS

♛ Keep It Cold
Butter, shortening, flour, even your hands — cold is key for flaky layers.

🌿 Gluten-Free Tip
Add ½ tsp xanthan gum per cup of GF flour for structure, and chill the dough even longer before rolling.

✂ Trim and Tuck
Leave a 1-inch overhang, then fold it under and crimp for a tidy, thick edge that holds shape.

Don't Overwork It
Mix until it just comes together. Visible bits of butter = good.

〰 Vent Wisely
Slit or score top crusts to let steam escape and avoid soggy tops.

◐ Blind Bake Basics
Dock the bottom, line with parchment, fill with weights. Bake 10–15 mins at 375°F, then remove weights and finish.

Grandma's PUMPKIN PIE

Just sweet enough, warmly spiced, and baked in the kind of crust that cracks when you cut it — this is the pumpkin pie that lives at the center of every good Thanksgiving memory. If your family doesn't already have "the one," this is about to become it.

We always made two. One for the table, one for breakfast the next day.

The Golden Rules

- Use real spices – Skip pre-blended - for fresher, bolder flavor.
- Don't overbake – A slight jiggle in the center = perfectly set.
- Maple magic – A splash of maple syrup adds warmth and depth.
- Crust control – Keep dough cold for maximum flake factor.
- Shiny edge? – Egg wash gives the crust that pro-level glow.
- Plan ahead – Pie slices cleaner and tastes better the next day.
- Extra credit: Serve with maple whipped cream - a unforgettable finish.

NOTES:

Pumpkin pie keeps beautifully. Bake it up to 2 days in advance and store covered in the fridge.

INGREDIENTS

- 1 unbaked 9-inch pie crust
- 1 (15 oz) can pumpkin purée
- 2 large eggs
- ¾ cup packed brown sugar
- 1 cup evaporated milk
- 1 tsp ground cinnamon
- ½ tsp ground ginger
- ¼ tsp ground nutmeg
- ½ tsp salt
- 2 tbsp pure maple syrup
- 1 egg yolk + 1 tbsp milk, whisked (for brushing)

- Servings: 1 pie (8 slices)
- Prep Time: 15 minutes
- Bake Time: 45–55 minutes
- Cool Time: At least 2 hours (for clean slicing and full set)

Brush the crust with egg wash before baking for a golden, glossy finish. It's the little touches that make it look bakery-perfect.

DIRECTIONS

- Preheat oven to 375°F. Place a baking sheet on the lower rack.
- Whisk pumpkin, eggs, sugar, milk, maple syrup, and spices until smooth.
- Roll out crust into a 12" circle, place in 9" pie dish, and crimp edges.
- (Optional) Brush edges with egg wash for a golden finish.
- Fill crust with pumpkin mixture. Smooth the top.
- Bake 45–55 mins, until edges are set and center slightly jiggles.
- Cool completely before slicing.
- Serve at room temp or chilled, with whipped cream.

APPLE PIE with CHEDDAR CRUST

Everything we love about fall — warm spices, tender apples, and buttery, golden crust — with a bold twist: sharp cheddar baked right into the dough. The result? A pie that's nostalgic and unexpected in the best way. Trust us — your guests will be asking for the recipe before the last crumb is gone.

Don't knock the cheddar crust until you've tried it — it's genius. The sharp cheese deepens the crust's flavor without overpowering the filling

NOTES:

Apple Pie Wins

- Cold is gold - Keep butter, cheese, and water ice-cold for a flaky crust.
- Stop mixing the dough as soon as it holds together — overmixing = toughness.
- Don't skip the chill - Chilled dough is easier to roll and bakes up beautifully.
- Use a baking sheet - Catch any bubbling juices.
- Cover crust edges with foil if they're browning faster than the rest of the pie.
- Let it rest - Slice too soon and you'll lose those gorgeous layers.

INGREDIENTS
- 2½ cups flour
- 1 cup cold butter, cubed
- 1 cup sharp cheddar, shredded
- ½ tsp salt
- 6-8 tbsp ice water
- 6 apples (sliced)
- ½ cup sugar
- ¼ cup brown sugar
- 1 tsp cinnamon
- 1 tbsp flour
- 1 tbsp lemon juice

Servings: 8 slices

Prep Time: 30 minutes

Bake Time: 50-60 minutes

Cool Time: 2 hours

Apple variety matters. Use a mix of Granny Smith Honeycrisp apples for balanced flavor and perfect texture.

DIRECTIONS
- Make the crust: Mix flour, salt, butter, and cheddar until crumbly.
- Add ice water until dough holds. Chill 30 mins.
- Toss together sliced apples with sugars, cinnamon, flour, and lemon juice.
- Roll out dough. Fill bottom crust with apples, top with second crust.
- Crimp edges and brush with egg wash (optional).
- Bake at 375°F for 50-60 mins, until golden and bubbly.
- Cool: Let rest 2 hours before slicing. Serve warm or at room temp.

MODERN TWIST on Tradition

Creative, globally inspired, and boldly reimagined dishes that surprise and delight

Thanksgiving is a holiday steeped in rhythm—rituals we return to, recipes we memorize by heart, and dishes that feel like edible heirlooms. We come back to them year after year, because they root us. They remind us where we've been, and who we've loved.

But what if this year, we stirred in something new?

What if we reached beyond tradition—not to replace it, but to expand it?

This chapter is for the curious. For the flavor-seekers, the spice lovers, the cooks who flip through their spice racks like pages in a passport. It's for anyone who's ever looked at the Thanksgiving table and thought, "What if we did it differently this time?"

Sidebars & Pro Tips

- **Flavor Fusion 101**
  How to Blend Cultures Without Losing Soul

- **Make It a Moment**
  How to Plate for Maximum impact

- **Tips for the Adventurous Cook**
  How to be bold!

What You'll Learn in This Chapter

- How to Reimagine Tradition
- How to Cook with Global Influence
- How to Balance Bold Flavors
- How to Start New Traditions

Thanksgiving, at its heart, is about abundance, gratitude, and gathering. That leaves plenty of room for creativity. Maybe this year's wild card dish becomes next year's must-have. Maybe your guests ask for the recipe before they ask for seconds. Or maybe it just sparks a smile and a story. Whatever happens—make room for joy on your plate. This is where tradition meets adventure.

> Go ahead. Riff on the classics. Blend your family's heritage with the flavors that make your heart race. Break a few rules. Try something bold.

- **Pomegranate-Molasses Glazed Turkey**

A bold, ruby-hued turkey glazed with tangy pomegranate molasses and warm spices like cumin and coriander

- **Kimchi & Chive Mashed Potatoes**

Creamy mashed Yukon Golds infused with the spicy, umami kick of fermented kimchi

- **Za'atar-Roasted Carrots with Tahini Drizzle**

Caramelized carrots tossed in za'atar and topped with a rich lemon-tahini sauce

- **Sweet Potato Gnocchi with Sage Brown Butter**

Tender homemade gnocchi pan-seared in nutty brown butter and sage

- **Chai-Spiced Pumpkin Tart**

Pumpkin custard meets chai spice in a buttery shortbread crust, topped with crème fraîche.

- **Maple Miso Brussels Sprouts**

Crispy roasted sprouts glazed in maple, miso, and rice vinegar

POMEGRANATE-MOLASSES *Glazed* TURKEY

Forget the dry, flavorless bird. This turkey is brushed with a tangy-sweet glaze of pomegranate molasses, garlic, coriander, and cumin, creating a deep ruby lacquer that's as flavorful as it is visually stunning.

Check for 165°F at the thigh for perfectly juicy turkey.

NOTES:

Turkey Carving

- **Let It Rest** 20-30 minutes
- **Sharp Tools Only** Chef's knife > serrated.
- **No Slip Zone** - Damp towel under carving board.
- **Legs First.** Cut at the joint, not the bone.
- **Then the Breasts.** Slice along the breastbone, then across the grain.
- **Wishbone Trick.** Remove it early. Carving's smoother.

This dish keeps the soul of the Thanksgiving turkey alive, but swaps out sage and butter for bold, global flavor. It's a perfect example of how tradition can evolve—not disappear.

Arrange the carved turkey on a platter drizzled with leftover glaze. Garnish with pomegranate arils, thyme sprigs, and thin lemon slices.

INGREDIENTS

- 1 whole turkey (12–14 lbs)
- 4 tablespoons olive oil
- Kosher salt and cracked black pepper
- 6 garlic cloves, smashed
- 1 lemon, halved
- 1 bunch fresh thyme

For the Glaze:
- ¾ cup pomegranate molasses
- 2 tablespoons honey or maple syrup
- 1 tablespoon ground cumin
- 1 tablespoon ground coriander
- 1 teaspoon smoked paprika
- 1 teaspoon grated fresh ginger
- Pinch of cinnamon (optional)
- ¼ cup water (to thin, if needed)

DIRECTIONS

- Prep & Stuff: Pat dry, season, and fill with garlic, lemon, thyme.
- Roast: 2 hrs at 325°F, basting occasionally.
- Glaze: Simmer glaze until thick.
- Glaze & Finish: Roast at 400°F, glazing every 15 min until 165°F.
- Rest: Let sit 20–30 min before carving and garnishing.

Servings: 8-10

Prep Time: 30 minutes

Cook Time: 2.5 to 3.5 hours

Rest Time: 20-30 minutes

KIMCHI & CHIVE mashed POTATOES

A bold twist on a comfort classic—creamy Yukon Golds get an umami-rich upgrade with the spicy, fermented bite of Korean kimchi.

blending classic mashed potatoes with the vibrant bite of Korean kimchi for a fearless twist on the familiar

NOTES:

Creamy Potato Secrets

- Yukon Golds are ideal: creamy, buttery, and naturally rich.

- Don't overmix! Overworked potatoes = gummy texture.

- For extra silkiness, use a potato ricer instead of a masher.

Flavor Matchmaking

- Global mash-ups work best when you pair bold with familiar

These mashed potatoes are anything but basic. Fluffy, buttery, and silky-smooth, they carry the warmth of tradition but deliver a jolt of unexpected flavor.

INGREDIENTS

- 3 pounds Yukon Gold potatoes, peeled and cut into chunks
- 6 tablespoons unsalted butter
- ½ cup whole milk (or more to reach desired consistency)
- ½ cup finely chopped kimchi (drained, liquid reserved)
- 1 tablespoon kimchi brine (optional, for extra tang)
- 1 tablespoon toasted sesame oil
- Salt and pepper, to taste
- ¼ cup snipped fresh chives (plus extra for garnish)

 Servings: 6-8 persons

 Prep Time: 15 minutes

 Cook Time: 20–25 minutes

 Rest Time: not needed

Prepare a few hours early and keep warm in a covered dish, or refrigerate overnight and reheat gently with a splash of milk or butter to restore creaminess.

DIRECTIONS

- Cook potatoes in salted water until fork-tender, 15–18 minutes. Drain well.
- Mash with butter and stir in milk until smooth and creamy. Season with salt and pepper.
- Fold in chopped kimchi, sesame oil, and kimchi brine (if using). Stir in chives.
- Taste, adjust seasoning, and garnish with extra chives and a drizzle of sesame oil.

Za'atar
ROASTED CARROTS
WITH TAHINI DRIZZLE

Caramelized, earthy, and dressed with creamy tahini—this side dish is a vibrant fusion of tradition and global flair.

Cooking globally doesn't mean complexity—it means curiosity on a plate

NOTES:

Carrot Secrets

- Use thin or halved carrots for faster roasting and deeper caramelization.
- Don't overcrowd the pan — space promotes crisp edges.
- Make the tahini drizzle ahead; it thickens and gets more flavorful with time.
- Add crunch with toasted pine nuts, crushed pistachios, or sesame seeds.
- Taste your za'atar blend first — adjust with sumac or extra sesame if needed.

INGREDIENTS

- 2 lbs carrots, peeled and cut on the diagonal (or use rainbow carrots for color)
- 2 tablespoons olive oil
- 1½ tablespoons za'atar
- ¾ teaspoon kosher salt
- Freshly ground black pepper, to taste
- ¼ cup tahini
- 2 tablespoons lemon juice
- 1 garlic clove, grated or finely minced
- 2–3 tablespoons water (to thin)
- Pinch of salt

Servings: 4-6 persons

Prep Time: 15 minutes

Cook Time: 30–35 minutes

Rest Time: not needed

DIRECTIONS

- Preheat oven to 425°F. Toss carrots with olive oil, za'atar, salt, and pepper. Roast on a parchment-lined sheet for 30–35 minutes, flipping once, until caramelized.
- Mix the Drizzle: Whisk tahini, lemon juice, garlic, and salt. Add water until smooth and pourable.
- Plate carrots, drizzle with sauce, and top with toasted pine nuts or pomegranate seeds.

Za'atar is more than a spice blend—it's a passport to the Levant. Traditionally made with thyme, sumac, and sesame seeds, it brings tang, crunch, and a sense of place to whatever it touches.

Sweet Potato GNOCCHI WITH SAGE BROWN BUTTER

A cozy, elegant dish that brings together earthy sweetness and nutty richness—handmade comfort with a gourmet finish.

These golden, pan-seared pillows of roasted sweet potato are soft on the inside and lightly crisped on the edges.

NOTES:

Gnocchi Success

- Cool the potatoes before mixing—hot mash = sticky dough.
- Less flour is better—use just enough to hold the dough together.
- Don't overwork the dough; gentle hands make tender gnocchi.
- Boil, then crisp—pan-searing adds golden texture and deep flavor.
- Sage butter is quick magic—watch closely so it doesn't burn

INGREDIENTS

- For the Gnocchi:
- 2 medium sweet potatoes (about 1.5 lbs), roasted and cooled
- 1 egg yolk
- ½ teaspoon kosher salt
- ¼ teaspoon nutmeg
- ¾ to 1 cup all-purpose flour (start with less, add as needed)
- Extra flour, for rolling
- For the Sage Brown Butter:
- 6 tablespoons unsalted butter
- 8–10 fresh sage leaves
- Pinch of flaky salt

This dish pairs the caramelized sweetness of roasted sweet potato with the rich, nutty savoriness of brown butter—an example of how to layer bold components for perfect harmony. The sage? It's the aromatic bridge between both.

DIRECTIONS

- Roast whole sweet potatoes at 400°F for 45–60 minutes until soft. Let cool, scoop out flesh, and mash. Cool.
- Mix cooled mashed sweet potato with egg yolk, salt, nutmeg, and flour until a soft, slightly sticky dough forms.
- Roll dough into ropes, cut into 1-inch pieces, and roll over a fork for ridges.
- Cook in salted boiling water until they float, then 1 minute more. Drain and let dry briefly.
- Melt butter in a skillet, add sage, and cook until golden and aromatic. Sauté gnocchi in the butter until crisp and browned.
- Plate warm with sage butter, flaky salt, and optional parmesan or lemon zest.

- Servings: 4-6 persons
- Prep Time: 30 minutes
- Cook Time: 10-15 minutes
- Rest Time: not recommended

Chai-Spiced
PUMPKIN TART

A lighter, silkier, deeply spiced take on the classic Thanksgiving dessert.

This tart is a beautiful reminder that a recipe rooted in memory can still be reimagined.

NOTES:

Pumpkin Tart Secrets

- Fresh Spices Make a Big Difference —use fresh cinnamon, ginger, and cardamom for the boldest flavor.
- Don't Skip the Black Pepper - a pinch adds subtle heat and depth to the warm chai blend.
- Shortbread = No Rolling Required
- This press-in crust is beginner-friendly, forgiving, and faster than traditional pie dough.
- Pull the tart from the oven when the center still jiggles slightly.
- Chilling overnight for maximum flavour.

INGREDIENTS

- Shortbread Crust:
- 1¼ cups all-purpose flour
- ½ cup powdered sugar
- ½ tsp salt
- ½ cup unsalted butter, melted
- ½ tsp vanilla extract
- Pumpkin Chai Filling:
- 1 (15 oz) can pumpkin purée
- ¾ cup heavy cream
- ½ cup brown sugar
- 2 large eggs
- 1 tsp vanilla extract
- 1½ tsp cinnamon
- ½ tsp each: ginger, cardamom
- ¼ tsp cloves
- Pinch black pepper + salt
- To Serve:
- Crème fraîche or whipped cream
- Optional: cinnamon or candied pecans

DIRECTIONS

- Mix flour, sugar, salt, butter, and vanilla into a soft dough. Press into a 9" tart pan and prick with a fork.
- Bake the crust at 350°F for 15–18 min until lightly golden. Cool slightly.
- Whisk pumpkin, cream, sugar, eggs, vanilla, and spices until smooth.
- Pour filling into crust. Bake 35–40 min until set at edges and slightly wobbly in center.
- Cool 2+ hours or chill overnight. Top with crème fraîche or whipped cream before serving.

- Servings: 8 persons
- Prep Time: 30 minutes
- Cook Time: 40-50 minutes
- Rest Time: 2 hours+/overnight

Creamy pumpkin custard meets the warm, aromatic blend of chai spices—cinnamon, ginger, cardamom, clove, and black pepper—all nestled in a buttery shortbread crust.

Maple Miso Brussels Sprouts

These Brussels sprouts aren't just a side dish—they're a conversation starter.

Sweet maple. Salty miso. Tangy vinegar. This dish is a masterclass in harmony.

NOTES:

Pair with savory mains like turkey or tofu roast. These sprouts also shine cold the next day tossed into a grain bowl or salad.

Pro Tips

- Don't overcrowd the pan — space = crisp.
- Roast cut-side down for max caramelization.
- Use white (shiro) miso for a mellow, slightly sweet flavor.
- Warm the glaze slightly if needed to help it coat evenly.
- Taste the glaze before tossing — balance with more vinegar or maple as needed.
- Add crunch with crushed nuts or seeds at the end.
- Leftovers = gold — reheat or serve at room temp in wraps or bowls.

DIRECTIONS

- Set oven to 425°F (220°C). Line a large baking sheet with parchment paper.
- In a large bowl, toss Brussels sprouts with olive oil, salt, and pepper. Spread cut-side-down on the baking sheet. Roast for 20–25 minutes until deeply golden and crispy at the edges.
- While the sprouts roast, whisk together maple syrup, miso, rice vinegar, soy sauce, and sesame oil until smooth.
- Remove sprouts from oven. Transfer to a bowl while still hot and toss with the glaze until evenly coated. Let sit 5 minutes to allow flavors to absorb.
- Transfer to a platter. Top with toasted sesame seeds, crushed peanuts, or chopped scallions for added crunch and contrast.

INGREDIENTS

- 1½ lbs Brussels sprouts, trimmed and halved
- 2 tablespoons olive oil
- Kosher salt, to taste
- Freshly ground black pepper
- For the Glaze:
- 3 tablespoons pure maple syrup
- 1 tablespoon white miso paste
- 2 teaspoons rice vinegar
- 1 teaspoon low-sodium soy sauce
- ½ teaspoon toasted sesame oil

Servings: 6
Prep Time: 10 minutes
Cook Time: 30 minutes
Rest Time: 5 minutes

Roasted to crispy perfection and tossed in a bold glaze of maple syrup, white miso, and rice vinegar, they strike that sweet-savory-acidic balance that makes every bite unforgettable.

How to Do a Fusion Thanksgiving

Blending cultures on your holiday table without losing the soul of the meal

Fusion isn't a trend—it's storytelling through flavor. It honors where you come from, where you've been, and who you're feeding—blending personal heritage with culinary curiosity to create a Thanksgiving table that truly reflects you.

Here's how to create a fusion feast that feels deeply personal —and deliciously cohesive.

Start with a Familiar Base - Choose a dish everyone knows
- Add cardamom or ginger to your sweet potatoes.
- Infuse your gravy with lemongrass and a splash of fish sauce.
- Take your pie crust global with matcha, black sesame, or espresso.
- The key? Make it yours, not random. Let each twist have meaning.

Think Globally, Cook Locally -Build flavor bridges using bold ingredients
- Cranberry sauce with gochujang, ginger, or orange zest
- Sweet potatoes with harissa, preserved lemon, or ras el hanout
- Tamarind-glazed carrots, soy-butter rolls, or miso-honey Brussels sprouts
- Use what's accessible, but cook with intention.

Balance Is Everything - Pair standout dishes with quiet companions.
- If your turkey is spiced and sticky with pomegranate glaze, serve it with something clean and fresh—like lemony greens or simple roasted squash.
- Let the bold dishes shine by surrounding them with grounding ones.

Honor Your Heritage - Fusion is not about erasing—it's about layering.
- Bring in flavors that reflect your identity, your background, or your curiosity. Mix your family's cooking traditions with flavors you've fallen in love with along the way.

Create a "Passport Menu"
Label each dish with a tiny flag or country name.
Print mini menus for each guest.
Invite your guests to travel the world—bite by bite.

Flavor Fusion 101
How to Blend Cultures Without Losing Soul

- Start with a classic base like stuffing or cranberry sauce, then swap one global flavor.

- Try: cardamom in sweet potatoes, tamarind in glaze, sesame oil in vinaigrette.

- Let each dish reflect a story: your roots, your travels, your tastes.

- Balance with simple sides. Every dish doesn't need to be bold.

Pro Tips for the Adventurous Cook

- Taste as you go—especially when using bold global ingredients.

- Toast your spices—it wakes up their aroma and flavor.

- Acid, heat, and sweet must be balanced—use citrus or vinegar.

- Label your dishes with origin notes to spark conversation.

- Keep one dish familiar for comfort amidst the creativity.

Make It a Moment
How to Plate for Maximum Impact

- Use white or neutral plates to make color pop.

- Garnish with fresh herbs, petals, or seeds for texture and contrast.

- Layer textures—crispy edges, creamy bases, toasted toppings.

- Add height with stacked or layered elements.

- Think of your table as a visual feast, not just a flavorful one.

Dietary Friendly Table

Vegan Mushroom-Walnut Stuffing
Savory, herb-packed, and deeply satisfying, this plant-based stuffing features sautéed mushrooms, celery, onion, garlic, and toasted walnuts folded into cubes of crusty bread and moistened with vegetable broth. A hit of fresh thyme and sage brings it home.

Gluten-Free Cornbread
Golden, crumbly, and just the right amount of sweet, this cornbread is made with a gluten-free flour blend and stone-ground cornmeal. Coconut milk and applesauce keep it moist without dairy or eggs, and a cast-iron skillet gives it those crispy edges everyone fights over.

Low-FODMAP Sweet Potato Casserole
Made without high-FODMAP ingredients like onions, garlic, or dairy, this creamy casserole uses mashed Japanese sweet potatoes, infused with olive oil, rosemary, and lactose-free butter. The topping? A crunchy oat-and-pecan crumble with maple syrup and a hint of cinnamon.

Keto Green Beans Almondine
A light but flavorful side made with blanched green beans sautéed in ghee and finished with toasted almonds, lemon zest, and a dash of smoked paprika. It's crisp-tender, clean, and keto-approved — without tasting like a diet dish.

Dairy-Free Pumpkin Cheesecake
Creamy, luscious, and completely dairy-free, this pumpkin cheesecake uses soaked cashews and coconut cream blended with maple syrup, vanilla, and pumpkin purée. Poured into a pecan-date crust and chilled until set, it's rich, silky, and surprisingly easy.

Whole30 Turkey Breast with Herb Gravy
This simple, juicy turkey breast is rubbed with olive oil, salt, pepper, and a mix of fresh herbs, then slow-roasted until tender. The drippings are turned into a velvety, gluten-free, Whole30-compliant gravy using arrowroot starch and bone broth.

Delicious recipes that meet specific dietary needs without sacrificing flavor

Gathering Without Barriers

The most meaningful tables aren't just beautifully set — they're thoughtfully made. Whether you're welcoming vegans, gluten-free guests, dairy-intolerant friends, or someone on a specific wellness journey, the heart of hospitality is making sure everyone feels seen, included, and well-fed.

This chapter is about cooking with care, not compromise. These dishes are not the "free-from" versions people politely push around their plates.

They're packed with flavor, layered with texture, and built to stand proudly alongside any classic. Whether it's a dairy-free pumpkin cheesecake that no one believes is vegan, or a low-FODMAP sweet potato casserole that tastes like pure comfort, this chapter proves that dietary-friendly can still mean crowd-pleasing.

Here, we're not just adjusting recipes. We're expanding the table.

Building an Inclusive Table

- Cooking for guests with dietary needs can feel overwhelming — but it doesn't have to be. Here's how to keep it joyful and manageable:
- Ask in Advance: Reach out early and kindly. A simple "Anything you avoid eating?" shows care and saves last-minute stress.
- Label Dishes: Use small cards or notes on the table to indicate dietary details: "Vegan," "GF," "Whole30," etc.
- Balance the Table: You don't have to make everything dietary-friendly. A few thoughtfully crafted dishes are often enough. Include a protein, a carb, and a dessert everyone can enjoy.

Low-FODMAP CASSEROLE SWEET POTATO

A cozy, creamy comfort dish designed with sensitive eaters in mind—flavor-forward, gut-friendly, and irresistibly good.

- Servings: 6
- Prep Time: 15 minutes
- Cook Time: 35 minutes
- Rest Time: 10 minutes

INGREDIENTS (Use Free-From)

- 2 lbs sweet potatoes
- 2 tbsp olive oil
- 2 tbsp lactose-free butter
- 2 tsp chopped fresh rosemary
- ½ tsp sea salt
- ¼ tsp ground white pepper
- 2 tbsp unsweetened almond milk
- ½ cup rolled oats
- ⅓ cup chopped pecans
- 2 tbsp maple syrup
- 1 tbsp coconut oil
- ½ tsp ground cinnamon
- Pinch of sea salt

DIRECTIONS:

- Preheat oven to 400°F (200°C). Place whole sweet potatoes on a baking tray and roast for 45–50 minutes, or until fork-tender. Let cool slightly, then peel and mash.
- In a bowl, mix mashed sweet potatoes with olive oil, lactose-free butter, rosemary, salt, pepper, and almond milk until smooth and creamy.
- In a separate bowl, stir together oats, pecans, maple syrup, melted oil, cinnamon, and a pinch of salt until well coated.
- Transfer sweet potato mash to a greased 8x8 baking dish. Spread topping evenly across. Bake at 350°F for 25–30 minutes, until the topping is golden and crisp.
- Let rest for 10 minutes before serving. Sprinkle with extra rosemary if desired.

Roast whole sweet potatoes with skins on. It deepens their flavor and saves peeling time.

Keto ALMONDINE GREEN BEANS

Bright, buttery, and crisp-tender—this keto-friendly classic gets a smoky update for flavor that shines without carbs.

- Servings: 4
- Prep Time: 10 minutes
- Cook Time: 15 minutes
- Rest Time: 5 minutes

DIRECTIONS:

- Add green beans to salted boiling water and blanch for 2–3 minutes. Immediately transfer to an ice bath to stop cooking. Drain and pat dry.
- In a large skillet over medium heat, melt ghee. Add sliced almonds and toast for 2–3 minutes
- Add green beans to the skillet. Toss to coat in ghee and almonds. Add lemon zest, smoked paprika, salt, and pepper. Sauté for 4–5 minutes
- Remove from heat. Rest 5 minutes to let the flavors settle. Finish with garlic-infused oil or a splash of vinegar if desired.

INGREDIENTS

- 1 lb fresh green beans, ends trimmed
- 2 tbsp ghee (or grass-fed butter)
- ⅓ cup sliced almonds
- 1 tsp lemon zest
- ½ tsp smoked paprika
- Sea salt and cracked pepper, to taste
- Optional: splash of garlic-infused oil or sherry vinegar

Flavor Upgrade: Finish with garlic-infused oil (FODMAP-safe) for extra savory punch without actual garlic.

GLUTEN-Free CORNBREAD

A crispy-edged, tender-in-the-middle classic—now gluten-free and dairy-free without sacrificing a single crumb of comfort.

- Servings: 8 wedges
- Prep Time: 10 minutes
- Cook Time: 25–30 minutes
- Rest Time: 5 minutes (to cool and slice cleanly)

INGREDIENTS (Use Free-From)

- Ingredients:
- 1 cup stone-ground cornmeal
- ¾ cup gluten-free all-purpose flour (with xanthan gum)
- 1 tablespoon baking powder
- ½ teaspoon salt
- ¼ cup maple syrup or honey
- 1 cup full-fat canned coconut milk (shaken well)
- ½ cup unsweetened applesauce
- ¼ cup olive oil or avocado oil
- 1 tablespoon apple cider vinegar

DIRECTIONS:

- Preheat oven to 400°F (200°C). Place a 9-inch cast-iron skillet in the oven while it preheats.
- In a large bowl, whisk together cornmeal, gluten-free flour, baking powder, and salt.
- In a separate bowl, whisk maple syrup (or honey), coconut milk, applesauce, oil, and apple cider vinegar until fully combined.
- Pour wet ingredients into dry and stir until just mixed. Don't overmix — batter should be thick but pourable.
- Remove the hot skillet from the oven, lightly grease with oil, and pour in the batter. Smooth the top and return to oven. Bake 25–30 minutes until golden and a toothpick comes out clean.
- Let cool 5 minutes before slicing into thick wedges.

Serving Idea:
Serve warm with whipped dairy-free butter and a drizzle of honey

Vegan WALNUT STUFFING MUSHROOM-

A savory, herb-packed classic reimagined for everyone at the table—no butter, no eggs, just pure flavor.

- Servings: 6–8
- Prep Time: 20 minutes
- Cook Time: 45 minutes
- Rest Time: 10 minutes (to set and slice cleanly)

DIRECTIONS:

- Toast bread cubes until crisp.
- Heat oil in a skillet. Cook onion, celery, and mushrooms until soft and golden, about 8–10 minutes. Stir in garlic, sage, and thyme.
- In a large bowl, combine bread, sautéed veggies, walnuts, and miso or nutritional yeast if using.
- Pour in broth a little at a time until bread is moist but not soggy. Season with salt and pepper.
- Spread in a greased 9x13" dish. Cover with foil and bake at 375°F for 30 minutes. Uncover and bake 15 more minutes until golden on top.
- Let sit for 10 minutes before serving.

INGREDIENTS

- 1 large loaf crusty bread
- 2 tbsp olive oil
- 1 small yellow onion, chopped
- 2 celery stalks, finely chopped
- 2 cups chopped mushrooms
- 3 cloves garlic, minced
- 1 cup chopped toasted walnuts
- 2 tbsp fresh sage
- 2 tbsp fresh thyme
- 2½–3 cups vegetable broth
- 1 tbsp white miso or 2 tbsp nutritional yeast (optional)
- Salt & pepper, to taste

Serving Idea:
Top with crispy fried sage leaves

Dairy-Free Pumpkin Cheesecake

A creamy, spiced, dairy-free dessert that is plant based.

- Servings: 8–10
- Prep Time: 25 minutes (plus soaking time)
- Cook Time: None (chilled to set)
- Rest Time: 4–6 hours or overnight

INGREDIENTS (Use Free-From)

- 1½ cups raw pecans
- 1 cup pitted Medjool dates
- ¼ teaspoon salt
- ½ teaspoon cinnamon
- 2 cups raw cashews, soaked overnight or in hot water for 1 hour
- 1 cup pumpkin purée
- ¾ cup full-fat coconut cream
- ½ cup maple syrup
- 2 teaspoons vanilla extract
- 1½ teaspoons pumpkin pie spice
- 1 tablespoon lemon juice

DIRECTIONS:

- Blend pecans, dates, salt, and cinnamon in a food processor until sticky and crumbly. Press into the bottom of a 9-inch springform pan.
- Drain cashews and blend with pumpkin purée, coconut cream, maple syrup, vanilla, pumpkin spice, and lemon juice until completely smooth.
- Pour filling over crust, smooth the top, and chill for at least 4–6 hours, preferably overnight, until set.
- Slice and garnish with coconut whipped cream or crushed pecans.

Roast whole sweet potatoes with skins on. It deepens their flavor and saves peeling time.

Whole TURKEY BREAST WITH HERB GRAVY

A simple, clean, flavor-packed centerpiece that fits Whole30 and paleo lifestyles without sacrificing tradition.

- Servings: 6-8
- Prep Time: 10 minutes
- Cook Time: 75-90 minutes
- Rest Time: 10-15 minutes

DIRECTIONS:

- Preheat oven to 375°F (190°C). Rub turkey breast with olive oil, salt, pepper, rosemary, and thyme.
- Place in a roasting pan and cook for 75-90 minutes, until internal temperature reaches 165°F (74°C).
- Transfer turkey to a cutting board and rest 15 minutes. Reserve drippings for gravy.
- In a saucepan, whisk arrowroot into bone broth. Add drippings and simmer until thickened. Season to taste.
- Slice turkey and drizzle with gravy.

INGREDIENTS

- 1 bone-in turkey breast
- 2 tablespoons olive oil
- Salt and pepper, to taste
- 2 tablespoons chopped fresh rosemary
- 2 tablespoons chopped fresh thyme
- 2 cups bone broth or chicken stock
- 1-2 tablespoons arrowroot starch
- Salt and pepper, to taste

Use fresh herbs for best flavor, or dried in a pinch, and pair with roasted vegetables or a bright citrus salad to balance the richness.

Leftovers
Reimagined

GIVE THANKS A SECOND TIME — WITH DISHES THAT MIGHT JUST OUTSHINE THE ORIGINALS

You've celebrated, feasted, and maybe even napped. But now your fridge is full, and the magic continues. This chapter transforms yesterday's meal into today's flavor-packed favorites — globally inspired dishes, brunch-worthy bites, and freezer-friendly spins, all rooted in the bounty of your holiday table.

Brunch & Breakfast Revival

Thanksgiving Breakfast Hash
In a skillet, crisp up chopped stuffing, shredded turkey, and diced sweet potatoes. Crack in a few eggs and cook until the whites are just set.
Top with hot sauce or herbs.

tuffing Waffles with Maple Butter
Mix leftover stuffing with 1 beaten egg. Press into a greased waffle iron until crispy. Serve with maple butter (softened butter + maple syrup) or top with a fried egg.

Pumpkin Pie Overnight Oats
Stir ½ cup oats, ½ cup almond milk, and 1–2 spoonfuls of pumpkin pie filling in a jar. Chill overnight.
Top with nuts or granola in the morning.

Sandwiches & Sliders Reimagined

Cranberry BBQ Pulled Turkey Sliders
Shred leftover turkey and mix with BBQ sauce and a spoonful of cranberry sauce. Pile onto slider buns with slaw or pickles.

Gravy Melt Panini
Layer turkey, stuffing, and cheese (or dairy-free alternative) on crusty bread. Grill until golden. Serve with a side of warmed gravy for dipping.

Mashed Potato Grilled Cheese
Spread mashed potatoes and cheese between two slices of bread. Butter the outside and grill until crispy and gooey. Optional: add greens or caramelized onions.

Freeze It for Later

Turkey Pot Pie Pockets
Fill pie dough rounds with turkey, veggies, and gravy. Seal, freeze on a tray, then bake from frozen at 375°F until golden.

Sweet Potato & Sage Soup
Blend roasted sweet potatoes, broth, and sage. Simmer and season with salt and pepper. Freeze in portions for easy reheating.

Leftover Lasagna
Layer mashed potatoes, shredded turkey, sautéed greens, and a quick cranberry béchamel (cranberry sauce + milk or broth). Bake until bubbly, freeze slices for later.

Fridge-Friendly Storage & Leftover Tips

The Art of the Remix Transform leftovers with balance in mind:
- Too heavy? Add fresh greens, citrus, or pickled veggies.
- Too bland? Add chili flakes, vinegar, or a squeeze of lemon.
- Too dry? Reheat with broth, gravy, or olive oil.
- Too rich? Add crunch with nuts, seeds, or fresh herbs.

"Leftover Kits" for Guests
- Stock up on to-go boxes or mason jars.
- Label with guest names or meal suggestions.
- Include reheating notes or pairings.

Tip: Use small kraft paper bags or twine to add a festive touch.

Fridge-Friendly Storage Chart

Item	Fridge	Freezer	Reheat Tips	Avoid
Roast Turkey (sliced)	3–4 days	Up to 2 months	Oven or skillet with broth	Microwave (dries out easily)
Stuffing	3–4 days	Up to 1 month	Oven or waffle iron	Freezing with too much moisture
Mashed Potatoes	3–4 days	Up to 1 month	Stovetop with splash of milk	Microwave without stirring
Gravy	2 days	Up to 1 month	Stovetop over low heat	Overheating (breaks texture)
Veggie Sides (roasted)	3 days	Not recommended	Skillet or oven	Freezing (turns soggy)
Cranberry Sauce	7–10 days	Up to 3 months	Enjoy cold or room temp	Microwaving (alters texture)
Pumpkin Pie/Cheesecake	4–5 days	Up to 1 month	Fridge or room temp	Freezing whipped toppings
Salads/Leafy Greens	1–2 days	Not recommended	N/A	Soggy, don't save

Beverage *Pairing* and Toasts

Wine Pairing by Course
You don't need to be a wine expert to serve great pairings. This section breaks it down by course, with approachable, crowd-pleasing picks that elevate every bite. From crisp starters to rich desserts, these wines complement the Thanksgiving table—no guesswork, no stress.

Cocktails with a Holiday Twist
Classic Drinks, Seasonal Flair
These festive cocktails blend timeless technique with bold, autumnal flavor. Think cozy spices, orchard fruits, and unexpected herbs—easy to batch, easy to impress. Perfect for raising spirits (and glasses).

Mocktails & Kid-Friendly Sips
Each drink offers a grown-up vibe with a festive twist, using seasonal fruits, warming spices, and beautiful garnishes.

5 Toasts to Start the Meal With Meaning
A good toast doesn't have to be long, formal, or perfectly polished—it just has to be heartfelt. Whether you're raising a glass with family, friends, or chosen family, these short toasts are designed to set the tone with sincerity, humor, and heart.

Perfect sips and heartfelt words to elevate your Thanksgiving table

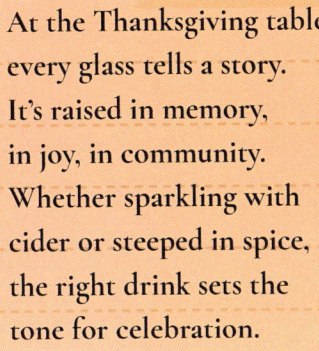

At the Thanksgiving table, every glass tells a story. It's raised in memory, in joy, in community. Whether sparkling with cider or steeped in spice, the right drink sets the tone for celebration.

Thanksgiving is more than a meal—it's a ritual of return. A day we slow down to share food, reflect on the year, and raise our glasses in gratitude. And those glasses? They carry more than liquid. They carry memory, joy, presence.

This chapter isn't just about what's in your glass—it's about why we raise it.

It's about finding the perfect sip for every guest, from your wine-loving aunt to the cousin who just turned ten. It's about crafting cocktails that celebrate the season, and offering non-alcoholic drinks that feel just as special. It's about honoring tradition while embracing play.

And when the drinks are poured, the moment calls for something more: a few words, well-chosen, to welcome, to remember, to celebrate. Here, you'll find toasts that don't feel awkward or overly formal—just meaningful enough to mark the moment. Because at the Thanksgiving table, every glass tells a story.
Let's make yours one to remember.

Build Your Own Mulled Cider Bar

Warm, cozy, and make-your-own
- Keep a large pot or slow cooker of mulled cider warm throughout the evening.
- Basic recipe: apple cider, orange slices, cinnamon sticks, cloves, star anise, and a splash of cranberry juice for color.
- Use mugs or heat-safe glasses.
- Add a small "How to Build It" sign with suggested combos.

Add-Ins

- Citrus Wheels – orange, lemon, or blood orange
- Fresh Fruit – sliced apples, pomegranate arils
- Sweeteners – maple syrup, honey, or cinnamon sugar rim
- Infusions – ginger slices, rosemary sprigs, or chai tea bags
- Spirit Boosters (optional) – spiced rum, bourbon, or brandy

Smart, sippable pairings for every plate

WINE PAIRING BY COURSE

Pairing wine with Thanksgiving doesn't have to be intimidating—oou don't need a sommelier certification to make great choices. All you need is a little guidance, a sense of your menu, and a willingness to pour what you actuallyenjoy. This course-by-course pairing guide gives you easy, crowd-pleasing wine options that enhance the flavors of each dish without overwhelming the table. Whether you're leaning classic or modern, plant-based or protein-rich, these wines play well with the bold, sweet, tangy, and savory notes that make Thanksgiving meals so memorable.

WELCOME SIPS

Light, fizzy, and festive— these wines greet your guests with a sparkle.

- **Prosecco** – Crisp, refreshing, and budget-friendly
- **Sparkling Rosé** – Bright with berry notes and gorgeous in the glass
- **Apple Cider** (non-alcoholic) – Seasonal and fun for all ages

Perfect with: cheese boards, olives, and mingling

> Pick one wine to carry through the whole meal, or mix and match by course. Either way, you'll be sipping smarter.

STARTERS & SALADS

Keep it light and zippy to complement fresh greens and tangy vinaigrettes.

- **Sauvignon Blanc** – Herbaceous, citrusy, and bright
- **Pinot Gris** – Slightly richer, great with fall vegetables

Perfect with: leafy greens, roasted squash salads, and light soups

MAIN EVENT: TURKEY & SIDES

The heart of the meal calls for versatile wines with structure and balance.

- **Pinot Noir** – Light-bodied red with earthy notes—ideal for turkey + stuffing
- **Chardonnay** – A full-bodied white that stands up to richness
- **Dry Riesling** – Crisp acidity to cut through buttery, savory dishes

Perfect with: roast turkey, mashed potatoes, stuffing, gravy, and Brussels sprouts

Tip: Look for bottles under 13.5% ABV—lower alcohol tends to play nicer with complex holiday meals

SPICED & SWEET DISHES

These wines stand up to sweet potatoes, glazed carrots, and bold autumn spices.

- **Gewürztraminer** – Aromatic, floral, and slightly sweet
- **Moscato** – Low-alcohol and gently fruity, great for balancing spice

Perfect with: sweet potato casserole, glazed veggies, and spice-forward sides

DESSERT PAIRINGS

Skip the coffee (or have both) and let your wine carry dessert home.

- **Port** – Rich and warming, perfect with chocolate or pecan pie
- **Late Harvest Zinfandel** – Jammy and indulgent with berry notes
- **Apple Ice Wine** – Bright, crisp, and naturally sweet—great with pumpkin pie

Perfect with: pie, cheesecake, and post-dinner cozy vibes

BUDGET BOTTLES THAT IMPRESS (UNDER $20)

- **Riondo Prosecco (Italy)** – Light, bubbly, and under $15
- **Kung Fu Girl Riesling (WA)** – Crisp with a kiss of sweetness
- **Bread & Butter Chardonnay (CA)** – Rich, smooth, and affordable
- **Underwood Pinot Noir (OR)** – Great in a can or bottle, ready for any table
- **Jam Jar Moscato (South Africa)** – Sweet, simple, and always a hit

COCKTAILS
WITH A HOLIDAY TWIST
Seasonal, sippable, and surprisingly simple

There's something special about a signature cocktail—especially one that speaks the language of the season.

BOURBON-CIDER PUNCH

Warm spice, crisp apple, party-ready. Best for: Welcome drinks, Friendsgiving, and firepit vibes.

Ingredients:
- 2 cups apple cider
- 1 cup bourbon
- ½ cup orange juice
- 1 orange peel
- 2 cinnamon sticks
- 3 cloves
- Sparkling water (to top)

Instructions:

Simmer cider, juice, and spices. Cool, stir in bourbon. Chill. Top with sparkling water when serving. Garnish with apple slices and cinnamon sticks.

Each one is easy to scale up, easy to garnish, and easy to fall in love with. Cheers to cocktail hour with a twist of

SPICED PUMPKIN WHITE RUSSIAN

Decadent, creamy, and full of fall A dessert-style drink with a cozy twist. Serve after dessert or as a final toast

Ingredients:
- 1 oz vodka
- 1 oz coffee liqueur
- 1 tbsp pumpkin purée
- ¼ tsp pumpkin spice
- 2 oz dairy-free cream or half-and-half

Instructions:

Shake all ingredients with ice. Strain over fresh ice in a rocks glass. Garnish with cinnamon.

PEAR-GINGER WHISKEY SOUR

Ingredients:
- 2 oz bourbon
- 1 oz fresh pear juice
- ¾ oz lemon juice
- ½ oz ginger syrup
- Dash of bitters

Instructions:
Shake with ice and strain into a rocks glass. Garnish with pear slice or candied ginger.

CRANBERRY SAGE GIN FIZZ

Ingredients:
- 1½ oz gin
- 1 oz cranberry juice
- ½ oz lemon juice
- ½ oz sage simple syrup
- Splash of soda water

Instructions:
Shake everything but soda with ice. Strain into glass. Top with soda. Garnish with a sage leaf.

Pre-batch cocktails without ice and refrigerate. Add garnishes and top with bubbles just before serving.

COCKTAIL HOW-TO: ESSENTIAL BAR TOOLS FOR THE HOME HOST

Want pro-level drinks without the pro-level gear? Here's what you really need:
- Cocktail shaker – (use a mason jar if needed)
- Jigger or shot glass – So you can measure with confidence
- Spoon – For herbs, fruit
- Fine mesh strainer – great for smooth pours
- Citrus juicer – Fresh juice makes a world of difference
- Ice bucket – Presentation matters—cold & classy

MOCKTAILS
& KID-FRIENDLY SIPS

Flavor-forward, grown-up feeling, booze-free options for all ages

ROSEMARY GRAPEFRUIT SPRITZ

Bitter, bubbly, and sophisticated enough for any adult palate.

Ingredients:
- ½ cup fresh grapefruit juice
- ¼ tsp honey or maple syrup (optional)
- Sparkling water to top
- Sprig of rosemary for garnish

Instructions:
Mix the above and serve over ice in a tall glass with a grapefruit twist.

HOT MULLED CRANBERRY CIDER

A rich, ruby-red alternative to mulled wine—fruity, spiced, and kid-safe.

Ingredients:
- 2 cups cranberry juice
- 1 cup apple cider
- 1 cinnamon stick
- 2 cloves
- 2 orange slices

Instructions:
Simmer for 10 minutes. Serve warm in mugs add an orange wedge innamon stick.

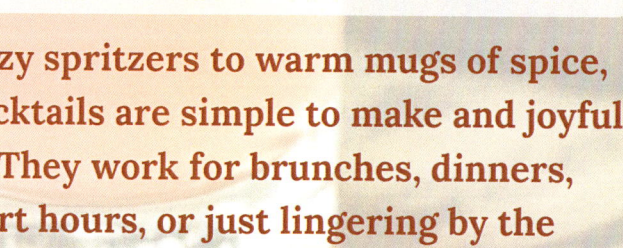

From fizzy spritzers to warm mugs of spice, these mocktails are simple to make and joyful to sip. They work for brunches, dinners, dessert hours, or just lingering by the fireplace. Cheers to everyone at the table.

SPICED PUMPKIN HORCHATA

Creamy, cozy, and completely dairy-free.

Ingredients:
- 1 cup almond or oat milk
- 2 tbsp pumpkin purée
- 1 tbsp maple syrup
- ¼ tsp cinnamon
- Pinch of nutmeg

Instructions:
Shake or blend until frothy. Serve over ice with a cinnamon stick.

APPLE THYME SPARKLER

Crisp, elegant, and perfect in a flute.

Ingredients:
- ½ cup apple juice
- 1 tsp lemon juice
- Sparkling water to top
- Fresh thyme sprig for garnish

Istructions: Pour into a champagne flute. Garnish with thyme and thin apple slices.

MOCKTAIL GARNISH IDEAS THAT WOW

Elevate any non-alcoholic drink with these festive touches:

- Herbs: rosemary, mint, thyme
- Fruits: frozen cranberries, citrus wheels, pomegranate seeds
- Fun Edges: cinnamon-sugar rim, salted caramel rim
- Extras: star anise, edible flowers, fancy straws or skewers

Freeze garnishes into ice cubes for a functional, beautiful touch.

5 TOASTS
TO START THE MEAL WITH MEANING
Short, sincere words that set the tone

A great toast is about intention. It's that moment when the table hushes, glasses are raised, and someone says something simple that makes everyone smile, laugh, or pause. These five toasts are written to be spoken out loud. They're easy to remember, and meaningful without being overly formal. Pick the one that speaks to your moment—or let them inspire your own.

- 1. The Gratitude Toast

"To hands that prepared, hearts that gathered, and the moments we'll carry forward."

Simple and heartfelt, this is perfect for opening a meal with warmth and intention.

- 2. The Family Toast

"Here's to the ones at the table and the ones in our hearts."

A gentle nod to presence and memory—ideal for multigenerational gatherings or honoring those not with us.

- 3. The Friendsgiving Toast

"Chosen family, full plates, and stories we won't tell our mothers."

Playful and real, this is a favorite for casual dinners and cozy circles of friends.

- 4. The Lighthearted Toast

"To stretchy pants and seconds without shame."

A toast for laughter and levity—because not every moment needs to be serious.

- 5. The Legacy Toast

"To recipes passed down, laughter passed around, and love that always returns."

A beautiful closer for anyone honoring family tradition, or simply feeling nostalgic.

Whether heartfelt or humorous, a toast gives shape to gratitude. It's the first bite of meaning before the first bite of food.

The Art of HOSTING

Welcome to the Table: Why Atmosphere Matters

Seasonal Floral Centerpieces
No need to be a florist—this guide helps you bring natural beauty to the table using seasonal blooms, produce, or even your backyard. Includes quick DIYs, arrangement tips, and a no-fuss way to keep things fresh (and fragrant, not overwhelming).

Curating the Soundtrack
Set the emotional tone with the perfect playlist—from prep to pie. This section walks you through crafting a soundscape that flows with the day, plus ideas for themed music moments and a linked Spotify playlist to make it easy.

Soulful Conversation Starters
Spark connection with questions that go beyond small talk. These 10 conversation prompts invite laughter, nostalgia, curiosity, and closeness—perfect for making the table feel even more like home.

Thoughtful Touches: DIY Place Cards & Menus
Details matter. Handwritten notes, playful menus, and easy printable projects help each guest feel personally welcomed. Plus, creative ideas for kids and last-minute solutions using what you already have on hand.

The Hosting Timeline: From Prep to Pour
Stay grounded with a flexible, sanity-saving timeline—from one month out to one hour before guests arrive. Includes key reminders, pacing tips, and what to do when something (inevitably) goes wrong.

Setting the Scene: Tablescaping with Heart
Learn how to build a beautiful, welcoming table with meaningful style—whether rustic, minimalist, or memory-filled. From linens and lighting to kids' table creativity, this section makes "setting the table" feel like setting the tone for joy.

Because the most unforgettable gatherings aren't Pinterest-perfect. They're human, warm, lived in. They smell like roasting vegetables and sound like old stories. They make people feel full long before the meal is served.

Hosting isn't just about the menu—it's about how people feel when they walk through your door.

IEvery Thanksgiving table tells a story. Maybe it's the mismatched dishes passed down from grandparents. The scent of sage or cinnamon wafting from the kitchen. The soft hum of jazz in the background. Maybe it's the moment someone laughs with their whole body, or the quiet glance between two people who are just glad to be near each other again.

Hosting is not a performance. It's an offering.

Atmosphere is the invisible ingredient. It doesn't show up on a plate, but it lingers longer than the best dessert. It's the light you set, the music you choose, the way the house smells when the door opens. And more than anything, it's the spirit you bring to the day—not trying to impress, just to express love and welcome.

You don't need a perfect house. You don't need expensive candles or professional tablescapes.

You need intention.
A sense of rhythm. A
nd a reminder that the goal is not control—it's connection.

Ask yourself:
- What do I want people to feel when they walk in?
- Where can I offer comfort, softness, or surprise?
- How can I let go of "perfect" in favor of personal?

SETTING THE SCENE: TABLESCAPING WITH HEART

More than décor—it's the first embrace of the evening.

Before the turkey is carved or the first toast is made, there's a kind of silent magic that greets your guests the moment they walk in: the glow of candlelight, the weight of a linen napkin, the way the table feels like it was set with them in mind.

Setting the table isn't about showing off—it's about showing care. A lovingly arranged tablescape invites guests to linger, to lean in, to feel held. Whether you go all-out or keep it simple, this part of the gathering offers an unspoken welcome.

THE BASICS: LINENS, LAYERING, LIGHTING

You don't need a designer's eye—just a few well-chosen elements to anchor the mood:

- **Linens**: A tablecloth or runner softens the space instantly. Don't worry if it's wrinkled or vintage—it adds charm.
- **Layering**: Mix textures—ceramic plates, cloth napkins, a sprig of rosemary, maybe even a handwritten menu.
- **Lighting**: Candles are everything. Tall tapers, fairy lights—use what you have to create warmth and glow.

Tip: Keep centerpieces low so everyone can see each other.

Set the Table the Night Before
The oven will be full, the kitchen will be chaos, and you'll thank yourself for the calm of waking up to a table already set. Pour a glass of wine, turn on some music, and treat it like a ritual. It's one of the most grounding things you can do.

MOOD BY STYLE

Every table tells a different story. Choose the one that reflects yours:

Rustic Harvest
Burlap runners, wooden chargers, dried wheat bundles, and copper or amber glassware. Rich tones like rust, mustard, and olive create a cozy, earthy vibe.

Minimalist Modern
A monochrome or neutral color palette, matte dishes, sculptural mini pumpkins, and a long line of candlelight. Clean and calming—perfect for those who love subtle elegance.

Family Heirloom
Mismatched plates, vintage silverware, old jam jars for flowers, and handwritten name cards. Infuse the table with memory and meaning. It doesn't have to match—it just has to matter.

KID'S TABLE MAGIC

Make the youngest guests feel like honored ones with:

- Paper placemats (drawn on or printed with games)
- Mini cups of crayons at each setting
- Thanksgiving trivia or jokes to read aloud
- DIY crown or turkey hat kits to keep hands busy before dinner

Pro Tip: A few minutes of setup can buy you a full hour of peace.

SEASONAL FLORAL CENTERPIECES

Bring the table to life—naturally

A great floral arrangement doesn't need to come from a florist. With the right seasonal ingredients and a few creative touches, your centerpiece can feel thoughtful, beautiful, and effortless. Whether you're crafting a statement piece or scattering a few natural accents, this is about bringing the outdoors in—on your terms.

THE BEST CENTERPIECES NVITE PRESENCE, SPARK COMPLIMENTS, AND SUBTLY TIE YOUR TABLE TOGETHER.

DIY: FIVE-MINUTE TABLE RUNNER

1. **Layer a base** of eucalyptus or fall leaves down the center of your table.
2. **Tuck in clusters** of small gourds, apples, or pears.
3. **Add texture** with dried flowers, pinecones, or cinnamon sticks.
4. **Finish with candles** (votives or tapers) nestled safely among the foliage.

Looks lush, costs little, and takes under five minutes.

A GUIDE TO SEASONAL BLOOMS & FOLIAGE

Focus on texture, tone, and seasonality. Here are some no-fuss options that feel fresh and festive for fall:

- **Eucalyptus** – *Elegant and soft with a subtle, calming scent*
- **Mums** – *Affordable, long-lasting, and available in rich autumn tones*
- **Dried citrus slices** – *Orange, lemon, or blood orange for color and texture*
- **Marigolds, zinnias, or sunflowers** – *For vibrant farmhouse vibes*
- **Grasses, wheat, or seed pods** – *Earthy and sculptural, perfect for layering*

Tip: Stick to 2–3 varieties per arrangement for a cohesive look.

LOW VS. TALL ARRANGEMENTS

- **Low** arrangements encourage conversation—your guests can see and connect across the table.
- **Tall** arrangements add drama but can block sightlines—better suited for buffets or sideboards.
- **Pro move**: Use tall, narrow stems that guests can see through if you want height without disconnect.

FLORAL TIP: KEEP IT FRESH WITHOUT THE OVERWHELM

- **Skip strong-smelling flowers** like lilies or gardenias that can compete with food aromas.
- **Trim stems at an angle** and refresh water daily for longer life.
- **Use flower frogs, chicken wire, or tape grids** to structure DIY arrangements without fuss.
- **Mist gently** right before guests arrive to revive wilting petals.

USING PRODUCE AS DECOR

Nature's bounty is your best styling tool.

- **Gourds and mini pumpkins** nestled among greenery
- **Apples or pomegranates** in a footed bowl
- **Cranberries in water** with floating candles in a glass vase
- **Dried orange slices** hung from branches or scattered on platters

It's edible, compostable, and seasonally stunning.

THOUGHTFUL TOUCHES:
DIY PLACE CARDS & MENUS

Small details that say: "I'm so glad you're here."

A menu doesn't just list the food—it builds anticipation. A place card doesn't just tell someone where to sit—it tells them they were expected. These small, simple gestures carry a surprising amount of emotional weight. Adding handmade or personalized touches to your table doesn't require a glue gun or graphic design degree. A handwritten note, a watercolor flourish, or even a printed coloring sheet for the kids can instantly make your gathering feel more thoughtful than formal.

These moments of creativity invite connection, spark conversation, and add that extra layer of warmth that says: this meal was made with more than ingredients—it was made with care.

Printable Place Cards & Templates

Use downloadable templates with faux calligraphy fonts or trace over pencil guidelines with a gel pen or metallic marker. Print on cardstock or cut-up kraft paper and tuck them into mini pumpkins, pinecones, or napkin folds. Tie name tags to a sprig of rosemary or cinnamon stick for instant aroma and style.

A Handwritten note It's a quiet moment that can mean more than any centerpiece.

Handwritten Gratitude Notes

Place a small folded card at each setting with a simple message inside. It could be a shared memory, a compliment, or just "Thank you for being here."

Creative Menu Displays

Let your menu become part of your décor.

- Mini scrolls tied with twine or ribbon at each plate
- Kraft paper runners with the menu written across the center of the table
- Watercolor tags clipped to a napkin ring or tucked under cutlery
- Chalkboard easel signs for a casual buffet-style layout.

Kid-Friendly Menu Magic

Keep little ones engaged with:

- Coloring menus (printable or DIY) with themed illustrations, tic-tac-toe, and gratitude prompts
- Crayon cups or mini packs at each setting
- Activity zones on placemats with questions like "Draw your plate!" or "What are you thankful for?"

Not only fun—it buys you time during courses.

No Time? Try This 10-Minute Setup Using What You Have

Fast, thoughtful ideas using what's already in your kitchen drawer:

- Tear kraft paper into strips for rustic place tags
- Use gift tags or business cards for name cards
- Write menus on index cards or small notepads
- Tuck a leaf under each fork with a name written in pen
- Use washi tape and a pen to label napkins or glasses

Reminder: A heartfelt scribble beats a Pinterest-perfect printout any day.

CURATING THE SOUNDTRACK

Let the music do some of the hosting.

Great music doesn't just fill the background—it fills the space between moments. It sets the tone before the first guest arrives, smooths transitions between courses, and lingers long after dessert.

The Thanksgiving table calls for music that's rich, warm, and human. Think acoustic guitars, slow soul, mellow jazz, or nostalgic indie. Music that doesn't interrupt, but invites. The right playlist adds texture to the room—like a second tablecloth you didn't know you needed.

THE THANKSGIVING PLAYLIST

Golden Hour Prep
Ease into the afternoon with warmth and rhythm. Norah Jones, Leon Bridges, Gregory Alan Isakov, or classic Van Morrison.

Background Chill
As guests arrive and conversation flows, keep things soft and steady. Bossa nova, lo-fi jazz, soft acoustic covers.

Gratitude & Gather (Meal Time)
Nothing too fast, nothing too sad—just easy, flowing sound.
Think: Bill Withers, Nina Simone, Iron & Wine, instrumental piano or strings.

After-Dinner Cozy Vibes
Time for flannel blankets, cider, and that second piece of pie.
Think: Fleetwood Mac, Hozier, instrumental soul, or smooth retro vinyl-style mixes.

MUSIC IS A QUIET FORM OF HOSPITALITY THAT SHAPES HOW YOUR GATHERING FEELS—WITHOUT SAYING A WORD.

> Don't overthink it. Hospitality is about intention not perfection

STREAMING TIPS & VOLUME BALANCE

- Keep volume low—just enough to fill lulls, never overpower voices.
- Place your speaker where it blends—not near the food or where people are seated.
- Test the vibe early while setting up—adjust as needed.
- Use crossfade or gapless playback to avoid awkward silences or jarring transitions.

The Thanksgiving Playlist

Build a mood that evolves with your celebration.

🟠 GOLDEN HOUR PREP
Ease into the afternoon with warmth and rhythm.
Norah Jones, Leon Bridges, Gregory Alan Isakov Van Morrison

🟢 BACKGROUND CHILL
Keep things soft and steady as guests arrive.
Bossa nova, lo-fi jazz, soft acoustic covers

🟢 GRATITUDE & GATHER (MEAL TIME)
Nothing too fast, nothing too sad – just easy, flowing sound.
Bill Withers, Nina Simone, Iron & Wine, instrumental piano or strings

🟤 AFTER-DINNER COZY VIBES
Time for flannel blankets, cider, and that second piece of pie
Fleetwood Mac, Hozier
instrumental soul, smooth retro mixes

THE HOSTING TIMELINE: FROM PREP TO POUR

Hosting doesn't have to be hectic—just paced with purpose

Throwing a Thanksgiving gathering is part cooking marathon, part love letter. And while spontaneity has its charm, a gentle plan is your best friend. This isn't about perfection—it's about pacing. A clear timeline helps you stay grounded, get ahead, and actually enjoy your own party.

1 Month Before
- Finalize your guest list
- Choose your menu
- Order specialty items (turkeys, gluten-free rolls, hard-to-find wines)

2 Weeks Before
- Set your decor vision (centerpieces, linens, candles)
- Test recipes if you're trying something new
- Shop for wine, spirits, or non-alcoholic beverages

1 Week Before
- Do a deep clean of entertaining spaces
- Grocery shop for non-perishables
- Pull out serving pieces, platters, and glassware

2–3 Days Before
- Begin make-ahead dishes (cranberry sauce, casseroles, dessert)
- Start fridge Tetris—clear space and organize
- Finalize playlist and place settings

Day Of
- Morning: Cook remaining dishes, prep the turkey
- Midday: Set out drinks, arrange flowers or foliage
- Late afternoon: Light candles, fluff pillows, take a breath

1 Hour Before
- Music on
- Apron off
- Drink in hand
- Doors open

WHAT TO DO WHEN SOMETHING GOES WRONG (BECAUSE IT WILL)

No matter how much you plan, something will go sideways. A pie will crack. A side dish might be forgotten in the oven. A chair might break (true story).

Here's what to remember:
- **Keep your sense of humor**—laughter makes a great course correction.
- **Invite help.** Let guests feel useful—it brings them closer.
- **Shift focus back to the table.** The conversation and connection are what last.
- **Improvise boldly.** Burned stuffing? Serve extra mashed potatoes with flair.
- **Let go.** A perfect moment rarely looks perfect.

10 SOULFUL CONVERSATION STARTERS

A warm, inclusive way to open hearts around the table.

1. What's a tradition from your childhood you'd love to bring back?
2. What's a meal or dish that brings back a memory?
3. Who's someone you wish could be at this table tonight?
4. What's something you learned this year you're grateful for?
5. What's your pie personality?
6. Name a "small joy" that made a big difference this year.
7. If our meal had a theme song, what would it be?
8. What's the most unexpected thing you're thankful for?
9. What would you title your life's chapter this fall?
10. Share a wish for the person to your left.

HOSTING ISN'T ABOUT CONTROLLING THE DAY. IT'S ABOUT HOLDING SPACE FOR JOY— WHATEVER FORM IT TAKES

CLOSING REFLECTION:
MORE THAN A MEAL

What we're really doing when we set the table.

Thanksgiving is never just about the food. Not really.
It's the act of gathering, of making space—for each other, for memory, for gratitude, for the present moment in all its messy, beautiful fullness. It's hands chopping, folding, lighting, arranging. It's someone wiping down chairs they only use once a year. It's a playlist playing for no one yet. It's a pie cooling on a counter while a child asks if it's time to eat.

This book is filled with recipes and rituals, but more than anything, it's a celebration of what happens around the food. The laughter. The second chances. The silence. The seat you save for someone who isn't there. The toast that surprises you with how much it matters.

You don't need a perfect table.
You need a welcoming one.

Because when you cook with intention and gather with heart, it ripples out. The warmth you create becomes a memory someone carries. The extra place you set becomes a story retold. The food becomes a legacy—not of dishes, but of care.

So here's to the late nights, the wrinkled napkins, the mismatched plates, the burnt rolls, and the full hearts.

May every Thanksgiving be less about impressing—and more about expressing love.

You've set the table. You've told your story.
Now let the people in.

Notes

Notes

Notes

Notes

www.ingramcontent.com/pod-product-compliance
Ingram Content Group UK Ltd.
Pitfield, Milton Keynes, MK11 3LW, UK
UKRC040330240426
12048UKWH00007B/94